# Christmas around the World

by **Emily Kelley**   *illustrations by* **Joni Oeltjenbruns**

On My Own
**HOLIDAYS**

Carolrhoda Books, Inc. / Minneapolis

*To my family and the memory of my dad,*
*and especially to Sam—E. K.*

*To my parents, Neil and Mary, for teaching me*
*the real meaning of Christmas—J. O.*

*This book is available in two editions:*
Library binding by Carolrhoda Books, Inc., a division of Lerner Publishing Group
Soft cover by First Avenue Editions, an imprint of Lerner Publishing Group
241 First Avenue North
Minneapolis, MN 55401 U.S.A.

Website address: www.lernerbooks.com

Library of Congress Cataloging-in-Publication Data

Kelley, Emily.
    Christmas around the world / by Emily Kelley ; illustrations by Joni Oeltjenbruns.
(Rev. ed.)
       p.   cm. — (On my own biography)
    ISBN: 0–87614–915–8 (lib. bdg. : alk. paper)
    ISBN: 1–57505–580–5 (pbk. : alk. paper)
    1. Christmas—Juvenile literature. I. Oeltjenbruns, Joni. II. Title. III. Series.
GT4985.5 .K44 2004
394.2663—dc21                                              2002004677

Manufactured in the United States of America
1 2 3 4 5 6 – JR – 09 08 07 06 05 04

# Table of Contents

# What Is Christmas?

Christmas is the celebration of the birth of Jesus. The story of Jesus' birth is told in the Christian Bible. The Bible says that Jesus was born more than two thousand years ago. A carpenter named Joseph and his wife, Mary, lived in Nazareth, a town in Palestine. Mary was about to have a child. An angel had come to Mary and told her that she would give birth to the Son of God.

At that time, Palestine was ruled by the Romans. The Roman emperor had ordered that a list called a census be made of everyone in the Roman Empire. So Mary and Joseph had to go to Bethlehem to add their names to the census. When they arrived in the town, there was no room for them inside the inn. But one innkeeper allowed them to

stay in a stable, where Mary gave birth to her son, Jesus.

Mary and Joseph made a bed for Jesus in the animals' manger. Shepherds came to see him. They said that angels in the sky had sung to them about this special baby. From far away, three wise men came to give him gifts.

Today, Christians around the world celebrate Christmas every December or January. In this book, you will find out about Christmas customs of eight countries. Some of these customs are ancient. Others are much newer. From one country to another, Christmas is celebrated in many different ways. But one thing is certain. Christmas warmth and joy are the same for Christians everywhere.

In Mexico,

Christmas is called Navidad.

The main celebration is the *posadas.*

"Posadas" means "inns."

For nine nights,

friends gather together for a parade.

They carry small figures

of baby Jesus, Mary, and Joseph.

They carry lighted candles

and sing Christmas carols.

Each night, one man or boy
pretends to be Joseph.
He knocks on a house door.
The house stands for
a Bethlehem inn, or posada.
"Can Mary rest here?" he asks.
"No," he is told.
"The inn is full."
After first being turned away,
everyone is asked in for a party.
The ninth posada is on Christmas Eve.
When Joseph knocks on the door,
he is told there is room
only in the stable.
Everyone comes inside right away.
They sing songs and say prayers.
The figure of baby Jesus
is put into a manger.

Then bells ring and whistles toot.

There is a big, happy party.

Afterward, everyone goes to church.

Each night of the posadas,
children play the *piñata* game.
A piñata is a jug.
It is often made in the shape
of an animal.
It is filled with toys,
candy, fruit, and gifts.
Each night, a piñata is hung
above the children's heads.
One child is blindfolded, given a stick,
and twirled around.
He swings three times with his stick.
Three misses!
Each child takes a turn until—
*Whack! Whack!*
The piñata is broken.
Everyone dives for the toys and sweets.

In Ethiopia, Christmas has its own sport.

People play genna only at Christmastime.

Genna is like hockey,

but it isn't played on ice.

Ethiopia is too hot for ice games.

Genna is played on a field.

Players hit a wooden ball with curved sticks.

Crowds cheer for their favorite team.

The winners dance through town,

singing a victory song.

Ethiopians don't give gifts on Christmas.

Families celebrate by going to genna games.

Children also get sugar as a treat.

Another way Ethiopians celebrate

is by visiting one of their country's

special churches.

These 13 churches are hundreds of years old.

They were carved out of solid rock.

Many Ethiopians go to the churches

for Christmas services.

The service is three hours long.

Everyone stands for the whole time.

When the service ends,

a cross is passed through the crowd.

People kiss it to show their love

and respect for God.

Then they go home and eat a feast

of spicy chicken stew.

In China, Christmas brings
a special glow.
Christians light their houses
with beautiful paper lanterns.
Their Christmas trees are called
"trees of light."
They are decorated with paper chains,
paper flowers, and paper lanterns.

Santa Claus visits China too.
He is called Dun Che Lao Ren.
Children hang up muslin stockings.
They hope that Dun Che Lao Ren will come
and fill them with presents.

Christmas season starts in Germany
when the Christmas markets open.
The markets are decorated with
lanterns and tree branches.
The smells of sausage
and gingerbread fill the air.
People buy handmade toys,
Christmas ornaments,
and Christmas trees.

The tradition of Christmas trees
began in Germany.
There are many stories
about the first Christmas tree.
One story tells about a preacher
named Martin Luther.
He lived during the 1500s.
Late one Christmas Eve,
he took a walk in a forest.
Stars shone in the night sky.
Snow covered the trees.
Martin Luther wanted to share
this beauty with his family.
He cut down
a small evergreen tree
and brought it inside.

To make it sparkle like the stars,
he put candles on the branches.
These candles were the first
Christmas tree lights.

German families buy a tree
a few days before Christmas.
On Christmas Eve,
parents decorate the tree.
They put cookies, candy,
and glass balls on the branches.
Sometimes they add candles or lights.
At sunset, children come in to see the tree.
The candles and lights are lit.
Everyone sings
Christmas carols.

At bedtime, many German children
try to keep their ears open.
They are listening for Kris Kringle. THE CHRISTKINDL
He comes through the window
to bring gifts.
When he leaves the gifts behind,
he rings a bell.
A ringing sound on Christmas Eve
means a happy morning to come.

A few weeks before Christmas in Lebanon,
Christians plant seeds in small pots.
They water the seeds and care for them.
By Christmas Day, the seeds have grown
into tiny green plants.
These signs of new life make beautiful
Christmas decorations.

Christmas morning is a time
to visit friends.
People drink coffee and eat almonds
covered with sugar.

Next comes church.

At the end of the service,

every person touches someone else

on the shoulder or hand.

Some people give

a kiss on the cheek.

This touch is called
the touch of peace.
It is a blessing that everyone
can take home.
After church,
the whole family gets together
for lunch and presents.

In Lebanon, stories say that Christmas gifts
are brought by a young camel.
One story says that the three wise men
bought a camel for their trip to see Jesus.
The camel's baby wanted to see Jesus, too.
He followed his mother across the desert.

When the little camel saw Jesus,
he was filled with happiness.
He began to bring people gifts.
Lebanon doesn't really have any camels.
But children still leave water
and grain on their doorsteps
for the Christmas camel.

In Sweden, Christmastime
begins on December 13.
This is St. Lucia Day.
St. Lucia was a brave young woman
who lived in the 300s.
Many people then
didn't like Christians.
Some Christians hid in dark
tunnels for safety.
St. Lucia carried food to them every night.
She wore candles on her head to light the way.

On St. Lucia Day, Swedes
celebrate the Festival of Light.
Long before sunrise,
the oldest girl in the family
dresses all in white.
She puts an evergreen wreath
with seven lighted candles
on her head.
She carries coffee and buns
to her family in their rooms.
On Christmas Eve,
the family has a special dinner.
They usually eat ham and fish.
Then everyone opens their gifts.
On Christmas Day,
they go to church
and relax afterward.

During Christmas season in Australia,
there are no pine trees
covered with snow.
There are no sleigh rides or snowball fights.
It is summer here.
The sun shines brightly all day long.

Christmas Eve is a time of light and music.
Families and strangers gather
in each city square.
They light candles.
Together they sing Christmas carols
until midnight.

On Christmas Day,
children wake up early
and eat a big breakfast.
After breakfast, they open the presents
that Santa Claus brought.
Some families go to church.
In the afternoon, many people take
picnic lunches to the beach.

Turkey and plum pudding
are favorite foods
for Christmas lunch.
Some people eat lobster
or have a barbecue.
Children build sand castles
and play games in the sun
all afternoon long.

In Russia, Christmas season
is called Sviatki.
It is a beautiful time.
Snow covers the land and trees.
People bundle up in warm hats and coats.
It is a season of high spirits and joy.
Russian children get their presents
on New Year's Day.

There are many tales about
who brings the gifts.
The most famous gift giver
is Grandfather Frost.
He looks like Santa Claus.
His granddaughter, Snow Maiden,
helps him give out presents.
Snow Maiden has long, blond braids
and a furry white hat.

New Year's Day is a time for winter festivals.

Artists carve statues out of ice.

Children wave sparklers and dance.

A huge New Year's tree is put up

in the city of Moscow.

It is like a Christmas tree.

People decorate it with large dolls

called peasant dolls.

Many lights are strung

through its branches.

Russians celebrate Christmas on January 7.
Many people go to church at midnight
on Christmas Eve.
Afterward, they march in a quiet parade
with torches and candles.

Christmas Day is a peaceful time.
Families spend the day together.
Like Christians around the world,
they remember the reason
for Christmas warmth and joy.
They remember the birth of Jesus
more than two thousand years ago.

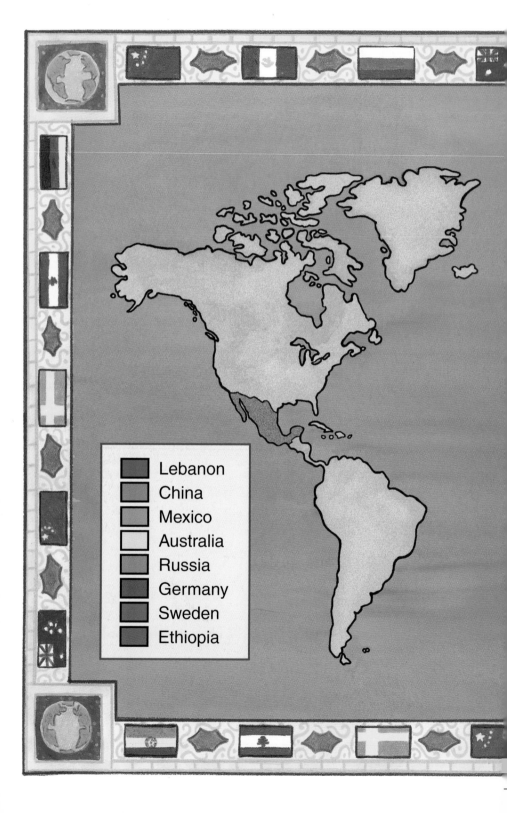

Lebanon
China
Mexico
Australia
Russia
Germany
Sweden
Ethiopia

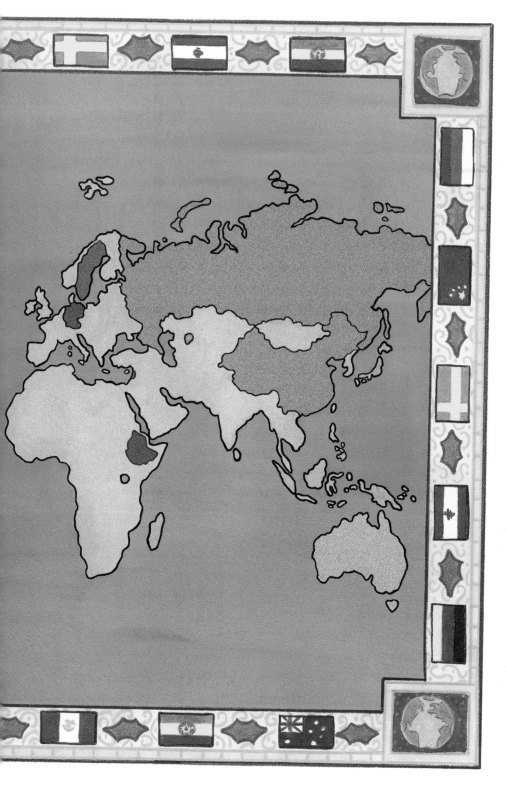

# Christmas Jokes

Q: What does Santa Claus say to Mrs. Claus when he looks out the window?
A: "Looks like rain, dear!"

Q: Why does Santa Claus go down the chimney on Christmas Eve?
A: Because it soots him so well.

Q: Why does Santa Claus have three gardens?
A: Because he likes to hoe, hoe, hoe!

# Christmas Tongue Twisters

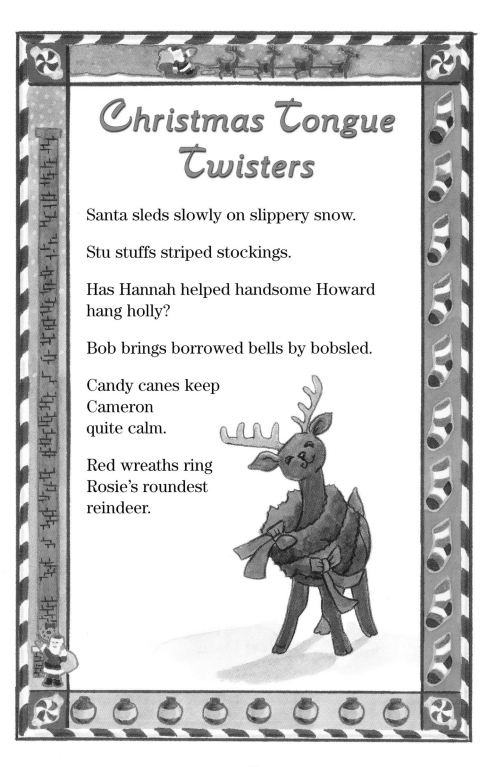

Santa sleds slowly on slippery snow.

Stu stuffs striped stockings.

Has Hannah helped handsome Howard hang holly?

Bob brings borrowed bells by bobsled.

Candy canes keep Cameron quite calm.

Red wreaths ring Rosie's roundest reindeer.

# Cornflake Wreaths

*Ask an adult to help you with this fun Christmas recipe. You will need:*

½ cup butter

3 cups miniature marshmallows

½ teaspoon vanilla extract

1 teaspoon green food coloring

4 cups cornflakes

1 tablespoon butter (for fingers)

waxed paper

red cinnamon candies

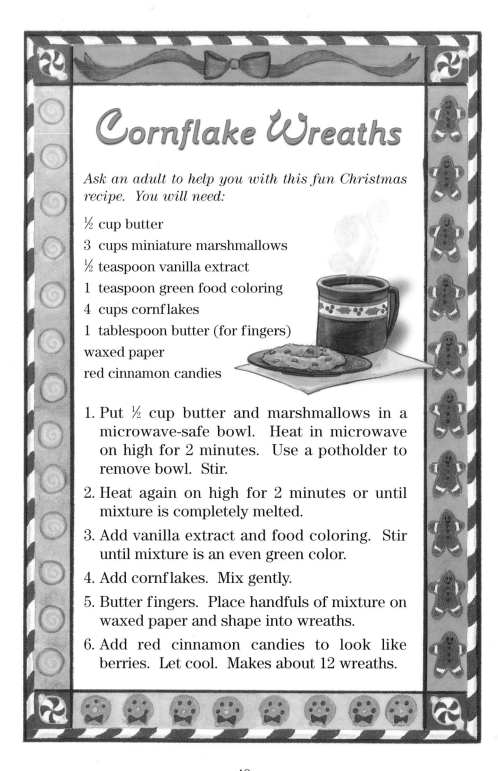

1. Put ½ cup butter and marshmallows in a microwave-safe bowl. Heat in microwave on high for 2 minutes. Use a potholder to remove bowl. Stir.

2. Heat again on high for 2 minutes or until mixture is completely melted.

3. Add vanilla extract and food coloring. Stir until mixture is an even green color.

4. Add cornflakes. Mix gently.

5. Butter fingers. Place handfuls of mixture on waxed paper and shape into wreaths.

6. Add red cinnamon candies to look like berries. Let cool. Makes about 12 wreaths.